ti

Recording the vision. Making it plain. That you may run.

Have I ever crossed your alley?

Have I ever paused on your road?

Have I ever noticed you?

Did you ever exist?

Have I ever washed your feet?

Have I ever looked in your eyes?

Have I ever said I care?

Samuel Lee

also from
FOUNDATION PRESS

A New Kind of Pentecostalism
promoting dialogue for change

Samuel Lee

For the Love of Hamoudi
my journey of faith into the Gaza Strip

Linda Todd Gharib

Israel Palestine
a christian response to the conflict

Craig Michael Neilsen

Blood Against Blood
for Christians only

Arthur Sydney Booth-Clibborn

Blessed Migrants

A Biblical Perspective on Migration

Foundation

Amsterdam | Singapore | Berlin | Portland

Other Voices...

"According to the Bible, every time God chose to bless and transform a powerful nation, He used foreigners and migrants—Joseph, Daniel, Esther, Paul, etc. I believe that the global revival will be ushered in by people whom God has sovereignly led to leave their native country in order to be invested in another country to see it move toward God's purpose and destiny. Samuel Lee has addressed this often-neglected truth in Blessed Migrants. I highly commend Samuel Lee and this book that undoubtedly comes from his heart."

Ed Silvoso
Author, Anointed for Business
President, Harvest Evangelism, Inc.

"In an hour when churches in the West are shrinking, God has poured out His Spirit on the nations of Africa, Asia, and Latin America. And now He is sending people from these regions of the world to reach Europe and North America for Jesus Christ. Samuel Lee, who immigrated to Europe himself from the Middle East, has discovered one of the Holy Spirit's key strategies for revival. I highly recommend this book to everyone who cares about world evangelism."

J. Lee Grady
Former editor, Charisma Magazine

"Blessed Migrants by Samuel Lee is a blessed book and a must read for everyone migrating through this life on Earth! People today are more mobile than ever before, and we all need a greater understanding of people in transition. This book will both educate and enlighten you to see migrants as God sees them. Dr. Samuel Lee is a modern-day teacher who gives facts and information to arm you. As a modern-day pastor, he reveals the Father's heart on this incredible topic. As a modern-day evangelist, he gives a strategy for soul winning that is revolutionary. As a modern-day prophet, he offers revelation on the topic and discusses the future trend he sees. Samuel Lee describes the Lord's blueprint for building nations through migrants. I recommend you read and give a copy of this important book to a friend!"

John P. Kelly
President
Leadership Education for Apostolic Development

Blessed Migrants

A Biblical Perspective on Migration

Samuel Lee

Blessed Migrants
A Biblical Perspective on Migration

© 2009 - 2012, Foundation Press. All rights reserved.

No part of this book may be used or reproduced by any means, graphic, electronic, or mechanical, including photocopying, recordiing, taping or by any information storage retrieval system without the written permission of the publisher except in the case of brief quotations embodied in critical articles and reviews.

Foundation Press is the non-academic division of Foundation University Press. Samuel Lee's books may be ordered through booksellers or by contacting:

Foundation Press
Post Office Box Box 12429
1100 AK Amsterdam
The Netherlands
info@foundationuniversitypress.com

ISBN: 978-94-90179-02-1

Unless otherwise noted, all Scripture quotations are from the Holy Bible, New International Version. Copyright © 1973, 1978, 1984, International Bible Society. Used by permission.

Scripture quotations marked AMP are from the Amplified Bible Old Testament Copyright © 1965, 1987 by the Zondervan Corporation.

The Amplified New Testament copyright © 1954, 1958, 1987 by the Lockman Foundation. Used by permission.

Scripture quotations marked KJV are from the King James Version of the Bible.

Scripture quotations marked NKJV are from the New King James Version of the Bible. Copyright © 1997, 1980, 1982 by Thomas Nelson, Inc. Used by permission.

Scripture quotations marked NLT are from the Holy Bible, New Living Translation, copyright © 1996. Used by permission of Tyndale House Publishers, Inc., Wheaton, IL 6019. All rights reserved.

design by | timmyroland.com

Table of Contents

Foreword One - Brother Andrew i
Foreword Two - Bishop Eddie C. Villanueva v
Introduction vii
Part One
  The Theology of Migrants 1
  Abraham, the father of all migrants 9
  Jacob, the cheating migrant 23
  Joseph, a forgiving migrant 33
  Ruth, a bridge-building migrant 41
  Daniel, a courageous migrant 47
Part Two
  Migrants and World Evangelizaton 55
  The Filipino Migrants 71
  The African Migrants 73
  The Korean Migrants 79

Conclusion 85
Bibliography 91

Foreword One

Brother Andrew
Author, God's Smuggler
Founder & President Emeritus of Open Doors

Never ask me to dedicate a church building for migrants in a restricted country—a land of persecution. Wally, my good Filipino friend, did just that. We met in Saudi Arabia, where on and off I had traveled and preached as much as I could. He, of course, lived there together with thousands of born-again Christians. Migrants!

One day, he asked me to dedicate their new church (I won't tell you where it was, but it was quite a big hall). How well I remember the event. I preached on Revelation 17, particularly on verses 13 and 14, in which all of the powers of evil unite to make war against the Lamb. No single power can kill the church, but united, evil forces think they have a chance.

Persecution, I said then, was not so much against us as people but against the Lamb of God, Jesus, who lived (and lives) in us. There was one thing, however, the enemy didn't know—he couldn't win! Jesus would win! The Lamb of God would win because He was (and is) Lord of Lords and King of Kings. Mind you, in the middle of persecution, not just in a glorious triumphant chorus, we would sing! Also, those called, chosen, and faithful would win because Jesus was (and is) in us. Yet persecution would not be pleasant. Much suffering would occur, and God would comfort and tell us, "This will only continue until the words of God are fulfilled" (Rev. 17:17). We had a great time. The next day, the Mutawa (religious police) came. They destroyed the interior of the room, furniture, and musical instruments. They also arrested the leadership. Wally ended up in prison, and after a mock trial, a judge sentenced him to death by hanging on Christmas morning. During his imprisonment, they interrogated, beat, and tortured him.

Time and time again—in what may have been an answer to his desperate prayer—he heard the words, "Until the words of God are fulfilled." One dark night— Oh glorious!—a bright light shone in his cell, and there stood Jesus. The Lamb! His Friend! Hallelujah! Jesus touched him. Jesus healed him. And after Jesus left him, Wally looked at his body. Even the ugly scars had disappeared.

I must admit that Wally was a bit disappointed. How could he later prove to his friends that he had been so badly tortured? Isn't that funny? The day before Christmas, the government suddenly released Wally and sent him home—the end of his migrant evangelism but surely not for others. The words of God had been fulfilled.

And my dear friend, my migrant brother or sister, you may not know it, but you are here in a certain country because the word of God is over your life. Is there a price to be paid? Yes. Is there a reward to be received? Yes. Yes. Yes.

You help fulfill the word of God. The Lamb wins, and with Him, the migrants and all of those who belong to the Body of Christ win.

Foreword Two

Bishop Eddie C. Villanueva
International President of Jesus Is Lord Church Worldwide

According to various published reports and studies, the Philippine government sends out more than a million of our nationals every year to work abroad through its overseas employment program. As a result, there are more than 11 million Filipino workers worldwide today. I would like to believe, however, that the actual number could be acutely greater than what is reported.

Because in my twenty-nine years of evangelistic ministry, in countries and places where I am commissioned by the Lord to visit or plant churches, I never fail to meet one of my own people. Yes, my beloved brown-skinned, small-framed, yet big-hearted countrymen who are highly favored for their integrity, intelligence, fluency, faith, and passion.

In the Philippines, they are hailed as our modern-day heroes. Because the money they send back to their families remains the biggest sustaining factor for our otherwise still volatile economy. But their greatness does not only lie in the money that they sacrificially eke out for their loved ones; it more so extends largely to the indisputable global influence they create—right where they are placed by God.

Yes, the Lord is able to bless His people even in a foreign land. Yes, there is an intrinsic blessedness even in being a migrant. Dr. Samuel Lee worded it so succinctly in this dynamic book, Blessed Migrants. There is an untold power that the godly influence of the Lord's faithful pilgrims in their God-designed destiny can unleash if they become the Josephs, Ruths, or Pauls in His kingdom. Surely, if we were as willing, we could also become powerful instruments in the hands of our all-powerful God, particularly in the global harvest of souls.

Yes, life, in itself, is a journey. Yes, each of us is a journeyer. I am certain that at one point in our lives one way or another, we all have become migrants. For migration does not only indicate simple geographical relocation; rather it does imply our seemingly unending search for our rightful place under the sun. Gratefully, the Beloved Son has paved the way for us to find it through the cross and by His sacrifice! Rise up, blessed migrant! We will pass this way only once. Make it count for the Beloved Messiah.

Introduction

There are approximately 150 million people who reside outside their native countries. We call these people migrants. Probably 33 percent of these migrants are, in one way or another, Christians, and maybe you are one of them. I am sure that you had a reason for leaving your home.

Maybe you are a domestic worker, a political asylum seeker, an economic migrant, or a war refugee, or you have another reason, which I cannot imagine or is too dangerous to mention in this book. This book will help you to understand that no matter where and who you are, God has blessed you, which makes you a blessed migrant! How are you blessed?

I am going to try to show you that in this book. Or maybe you are not a migrant but a host of migrants. You see your country mixed with people from different ethnic backgrounds and with different skin colors, religions, and languages. This book can help you to understand, especially biblically, the role of migrants in your society. In case you are not a Christian and you follow another faith or you do not ascribe to a faith at all, don't feel excluded! Even though the stories in this book are from the Bible, they still portray the realities of human life. Therefore, the book shares universal principles that will help you become a successful migrant or host. Whether you are from metro Manila, Philippines; downtown Abuja, Nigeria; or Kumasi, Ghana, and ended up in Europe, Japan, or the United States, you can use the principles in this book to become a successful migrant and a blessing to your host nation.

In part I, I discuss the role of biblical migrants. Who were the migrants in the Bible? Why did they migrate? What were their life conditions when they migrated, and how did those conditions develop later? Hopefully, between the lines of these magnificent biblical stories, you can discover your own story and realize that you are a modern-day Abraham, Joseph, Jacob, and Ruth.

In part II, I focus on today's migrants. Who are they? Why do they travel abroad? What is their role in God's plan for evangelization of the world? What are the biblical conditions for a migrant to be blessed, and how should a Christian migrant deal with other cultures and host nations? Last, what are the roles of host nations and the body of Christ in regard to migrants? Each chapter describes a migrant-exporting nation and can be used as a case study. I hope you discover your role in God's kingdom by becoming an instrument of love and a blessing to others.

Samuel Lee
A Blessed Migrant

Part One

Migrants in the Bible

Blessed Migrants

The Theology of Migrants

God has His own statement about migrants. He loves them. He cares for them and asks you to do the same. God's desire for migrants can be summarized in five major points in the Bible:

> God has a special love for migrants.
> *(Deut. 10:18)*
>
> They should not be oppressed.
> *(Exod. 22:21; Lev. 19:33-34)*
>
> Migrants should enjoy equal protection.
> *(Lev. 24:22; 25:35, Deut. 1:16-17; 24:17-21)*
>
> Migrants should have the chance to share equal responsibilities.
> *(Exod. 20:8-10; Num. 15:14-16)*
>
> God condemns nations whenever they oppress migrants.
> *(Ps. 94:6, Ezek. 22:7, 29)*

In Deuteronomy, God explicitly shows His love of migrants, "Yet the LORD set his affection on your forefathers and loved them, and he chose you, their descendants, above all the nations, as it is today. Circumcise your hearts, therefore, and do not be stiff-necked any longer. For the LORD your God is God of gods and Lord of lords, the great God, mighty and awesome, who shows no partiality and accepts no bribes. He defends the cause of the fatherless and the widow, and loves the alien (migrant), giving him food and clothing. And you are to love those who are aliens, for you yourselves were aliens in Egypt. Fear the Lord your God and serve him. Hold fast to him and take your oaths in his name". *(Deut. 10:15–20, emphasis added)*

God spoke to the Israelites not to be stiff-necked, and they have to remember where they had come from— that they once had been migrants in Egypt. God's love of migrants is regardless who they are, what they believe, or what ethnic background they come from. God loves migrants, and He hears their hearts when they pray to Him. God's words in the Bible are also for today. Every nation and every people should be aware of their past, and God wanted to remind the Israelites about their past in Egypt. Europe, for instance, has World War II, where men and women had to flight, hide, and suffer during those days in the past. What Hitler did to those nations is beyond imagination. Yet today many in Europe, especially the governments and lawmakers, forget that injustice and the cruelties of evil once oppressed them. They forget that they too once had to run away. What breaks my heart the most is how some migrants treat each other. Discrimination and racism are not only matters of black and white because those feelings can run very strong within ethnic groups. For instance, it astonishes me how people from different tribes in the same African country discriminate against each other.

It can cause huge problems if a migrant's child chooses to marry a person from another tribe. It astonishes me even more that people with those types of prejudices can call themselves Christians.

Also in Europe, I notice that some migrants from the same ethnic background become each other's stumbling blocks, due to jealousy, envy, and rage. Some people, who have a resident permit or a green card, feel as though they are superior to their fellow countrymen who are illegal. This is shameful. You cannot demand respect and equal treatment from a hosting nation when you are discriminating against your own countrymen. God told Israelites that they had to remember their past and that they too were once migrants in Egypt. This command from God is valid today for all of us.

Second, God demands that every nation not to oppress their migrants. "When an alien (migrant) lives with you in your land, do not mistreat him. The alien living with you must be treated as one of your native-born. Love him as yourself, for you were aliens in Egypt. I am the Lord your God". *(Lev. 19:33-34, emphasis added)*

Migrants should enjoy equal rights and not be mistreated. This is a command of God. Sometimes people treat migrants as third-class citizens; because they are foreigners, they are paid less and have no rights, especially when they are illegal. This problem has a history in America, and the United States has to remember what slavery did to the country. From approximately 1619 to 1865, almost 250 years, slavery boosted the American economy. The American economy avoided paying the salaries, of a portion of its work force, which allowed the economy to flourish. Think about it: if I have a business with two hundred employees who work for me for free, I will save a lot of money and be able to build up my personal wealth. Today, there are some just as serious examples.

Domestic migrants who work in Europe are often women from the Philippines, South America, African countries, or other nations who babysit the children of the upper class. But because they are undocumented immigrants, they do not have rights to defend themselves if someone treats them unjustly. I personally fight for those migrants' rights, and sometimes they are treated as if they were criminals! Many are your Christian brothers and sisters. (If you are a migrant under these circumstances, pray and be assured that God hears your prayers and knows your tears. Also, try to network with organizations that help migrants, and they might be able to help you.) Third, the Bible is clear that there should be equal rights between natives and migrants. It is a biblical commandment to protect migrants legally. Governments should not discriminate when it comes to practicing law and fulfilling justice. According to the law, the migrants are equals, but in practice, this is often neglected. "You are to have the same law for the alien and the native-born. I am the Lord your God". *(Lev. 24:22)* At the same time, migrants should not abuse their right to equality. Often, I have to counsel migrants who are trying to abuse the system. Those kinds of people lead governments to become more strict, and as a result, it affects many innocent and decent migrants.

Fourth, migrants should have the chance for equal responsibilities. "For the generations to come, whenever an alien or anyone else living among you presents an offering made by fire as an aroma pleasing to the Lord, he must do exactly as you do. The community is to have the same rules for you and for the alien living among you; this is a lasting ordinance for the generations to come. You and the alien shall be the same before the Lord: The same laws and regulations will apply both to you and to the alien living among you". *(Num. 15:14-16)*

Migrants have to participate in every one of the host nation's social responsibilities, so they have the opportunity to serve the nation in which they hold equal rights. Finally, God is very clear that the nations that are not migrant-friendly will be judged and condemned whenever they oppress migrants. God despises the migrant-oppressing nations, and eventually, these nations will reap what they have sown. "In you they have treated father and mother with contempt; in you they have oppressed the alien and mistreated the fatherless and the widow" *(Ezek. 22:7)*, and "The people of the land practice extortion and commit robbery; they oppress the poor and needy and mistreat the alien, denying them justice". *(Ezek. 22:29)*

It is clear that God is the God of migrants, and He defends suffering migrants, who cannot defend themselves when someone oppresses, abuses, or hurts them. God stands for them, regardless of race or religion, and God watches the nations to see how they treat their migrants. Nevertheless, God demands that the migrants are honest and respect their host nations. If not, why are they living there? Sometimes, I walk in some districts in Amsterdam, and to my deepest regret, I see foreigners, especially the youth, brutally treating elderly people or women by bullying them. Some Dutch people do not walk in those neighborhoods because they are afraid of being intimidated, robbed, or molested. This is unacceptable. This is the theology of migrants; this is what God demands that all of us—migrants and host nationals—universally do.

The Migrant Personalities in the Bible

The Bible is a book of migrants. Magnificent stories of great men and women of faith who were once migrants fill it. They are empowering testimonies of lives who can be examples for many today. Abraham, Jacob, Joseph and his brothers, Moses, Naaman's maidservant, Ruth, Ezra, Nehemiah, Esther, Daniel, Jesus, Paul, and the apostles were all migrants. Each of them had their own reasons to leave.

For instance, Jacob had to leave his father's house because he had cheated his brother and lied to his father. Joseph's brothers betrayed and sold him as a slave. They later took refuge in Egypt because of the drought and hunger in Canaan. Moses murdered an Egyptian and fled. Naaman's maidservant was taken captive in war. Ruth traveled in grief because of her husband's death. Ezra, Nehemiah, and Esther lived in captivity. Jeremiah and Daniel were captives in war. Who were they? Why did they immigrate? Where did they go, and what happened to them? After looking at all of these great personalities, it becomes clear that they all entered their new lands under different conditions; however, in the end, God blessed the majority of them, and they became successful. In this book, we look at the secrets of their blessings. Among all of these biblical personalities, Abraham had a holy task to leave his father's land and go to a place where God was leading him. He is one of the few people among these personalities, who did not leave because of economic, political, or familial reasons.

He left because God spoke to him and commissioned him to leave. Therefore, I call Abraham not only the "Father of the Nations" but also the "Father of All Migrants." The coming chapters analyze the lives of some of these great men and women. Furthermore, we will place their stories in the current world situation and try to learn important lessons for the today's church.

Blessed Migrants

Abraham, the father of all migrants

Christians, Jews, and Muslims all agree on Abraham (aka Abram). They all consider him to be the "Father of All Nations." The LORD spoke to Abram, "Leave your country, your people and your father's household and go to the land I will show you ". *(Gen. 12:1)*

As I mentioned earlier, he is also considered the "Father of All Migrants" because he started his life in the Lord with a journey of obedience and courage to a land he did not know. Abraham was a type of migrant who voluntarily decided to follow the Lord's command and leave his country and family.

He was a pioneer of faith who experienced adventure. It is essential to begin with Abraham because Abraham's life is the basis of this book's foundation. When God commanded Abraham to leave his homeland, He gave Abraham four important and life-lasting promises in Genesis 12:1–4:

> I will make you a great nation and will bless you.
> I will make your name great, and you will be a blessing. I will bless those who bless you and curse those who curse you.

Everyone will be blessed through you

Abraham was blessed with those four promises prior to his journey. I call them the migrant's blessings. They are not only for Abraham the migrant but also for many other migrants who came after Abraham, including those who live today. In other words, these four blessings are still valid for those who are Abraham's off-spring simply because of God's unchangeable blessings.

Even though Abraham traveled out of obedience, for which God blessed him, these promises are also for those who have traveled for motivations other than a godly call in their lives.

For example, Jacob's lies motivated him to leave his family and homeland, yet because of Abraham and God's promise to him, God blessed Jacob. After Jacob ran away from his father, he had a dream at Bethel. God spoke to Jacob and said, "I am the LORD, the God of your father Abraham and the God of Isaac.

I will give you and your descendants the land on which you are lying. Your descendants will be like the dust of the earth, and you will spread out to the west and the east, the north and to the south. All peoples on earth will be blessed through you and your off-spring . . . " *(Gen. 28:13–15)*

God blessed Jacob based upon what He had already promised to Abraham. This is important because there is a link between God calling Abraham to leave his land and Jesus asking Christians to go to the nations and preach the gospel!

Both commands are from God; both commands promote migration. Because through faith, you are the children of Abraham and through Christ the children of God the Father, the four blessings given to Abraham are yours today. You can combine them with all of the authority and power that Jesus has given to you. Let's look specifically at each promise and what it can mean for modern-day migrants when connected with the power of the Savior.

I Will Make You a Great Nation

When Abraham left his country, he was seventy-five years old, married to Sarah, and had no children—even though God had promised he would be a "great nation." God destined Abraham for greatness even though he did not have much to offer. The first blessing for a migrant is the same: a migrant is destined to be a "great nation," especially when they are in Christ and have chosen to follow His way. As migrants, you obey the Lord's voice in your lives and go to the nations to which God asks you to go. And you know that through His Spirit, once you go, you will be blessed in that nation.

As Abraham arrived in Canaan, he stood; looked at the land, the people, and the culture; and heard the language. As he was standing in the middle of all of these Canaanites, God promised to make him a great nation. Plus, He said that He would give the land of Canaan to Abraham's offspring. *(Gen. 12:7)*

How much land did the Canaanites occupy compared to Abraham's family when God made that promise? Abraham's group perhaps occupied five thousand square meters, but the Canaanites occupied their entire land! Yet God still said to Abraham, "This is yours! Even though you do not possess it now, out of you a nation will be born to whom I will give this land."

God has ordained every migrant called by God with a spiritual jurisdiction in the nation to which he or she has immigrated. It is God's will for that person to be there, and once the migrant understands the purpose of God in his or her life, then God releases authority and power to that person to act in that land.

Therefore, the believers in a host nation have to understand that migrants in their nation are potential blessings and the key to revival in a hosting land. I have met many great men and women of God who had heard His calling to leave their nations in Africa to come to Europe. Miraculously against all cir- cumstances like a lack of money or visa barriers, God still opened the door for them to evangelize in those host nations that once had colonized them. I also have met many migrants who were never called by God to leave their nations. They just left because of many personal reasons— some political, some economic, and some familial or work-related reasons. They were not even believers, yet in a foreign landamong foreign people, they met Christ, and now the Lord is blessing them in many ways. At the same time, they are strongly used to reach their host nation for Christ. There is a promise in the book of Isaiah to the foreigners who decide to follow the Lord:

> Let no foreigner who has bound himself to the LORD say, "The LORD will surely exclude me from his people." And let not any eunuch com-

plain, "I am only a dry tree" . . . And foreigners who bind themselves to the LORD to serve Him, to love the name of the LORD and worship him, all who keep the Sabbath without desecrating it and who hold fast to my covenant—these I will bring to my holy mountain and give them joy in my house of prayer. Their burnt offerings and sacrifices will be accepted on my altar; for my house will be called the house of prayer for all nations. *(Isa. 56:3-7)*

This is a great promise to all who have once decided to leave their nation for any reason. If these foreigners bind themselves to the Lord and worship His name in a foreign land, giving their lives to Christ, God will transform them from an ordinary migrant into a blessed migrant.

God also promises that He will listen to the prayers of these blessed foreigners. God extra anoints, accepts, and ordains the prayers of a blessed migrant. Blessed migrants pray blessed prayers! Blessed prayers bring forth great fruit. The first promise of the Lord to Abraham was that He would make him a great nation. In the same way, He will make those migrants who believe in Christ a great nation! For instance, when the brothers of Joseph entered Egypt, they were only a small group, but God blessed them, and the Israelites became a great nation within a nation!

They prospered and became a threat to the Egyptians; therefore, Pharaoh made them slaves. A migrant believer belongs to the Lord's nation. Therefore, God destines the migrant believer to advance the kingdom of God in the host nation (aka evangelism). This means saving souls through Christ and increasing the number of spiritual children in God's kingdom.

That's why migrant leaders head most of the largest churches in Europe. Ukraine has one of the largest churches in Europe. About twenty thousand believers are worshipping the Lord under the leadership of a Nigerian pastor, Sunday Adelaja. In the United Kingdom, pastors from Africa head some of the largest churches. This also happens in other developed countries. A pastor originally from Surinam heads Maranatha, a ministry that is considered one of the largest churches in Amsterdam. In the United States, African American ministers head some of the largest churches.

I have also met migrant believers who are not in a pulpit ministry, but they still have a great impact on the lives of those around them. I know a Filipino domestic worker in Holland who has prayed for a few of her Dutch employers. Although they had fertility troubles, through her prayers they conceived children. This Filipino lady, even though she was a migrant doing hard work, had enough friends from the host land that one day when she became sick and did not have insurance or enough money to pay for the operation she needed to have, all of her employers, for whom she had prayed, paid for her operation. Truly, God made her a "great nation."

I Will Make Your Name Great

This is the second blessing that God promised to Abraham. Blessed migrants are also entitled to this great promise. When Abraham left his country and entered strange nations, he was totally unknown. No one knew him, yet God gave him a great name and made him the "Father of All Nations." He also became a blessing to others, not only to his fellow tribesmen. You have to realize that God destines a blessed migrant for greatness and that he or she is sent to be a blessing to the people in the host nation.

There is a special anointing on the blessed migrants to bless their host land. Today, there are millions of believing migrants whom God has anointed to be a blessing to the nations they are in. They are to be an instrument of love, blessing, and care for their host nations. They can do this in many ways: through practicing their skills, sharpening their knowledge, and developing their talents as best as they can. If you are a migrant or a second or third-generation migrant, then I challenge you to know that you are destined to bless the nation where you live.

You are by all means a problem solver, regardless of how insignificant that problem might seem to others. I know a brother from Ghana named Thomas. Thomas is a cleaner. His life conditions are not so good; he lives under hard circumstances in Europe, yet he is a blessing to his employers. As he cleans houses, he also prays for each family. He prays for their well-being. He often talks to them and listens to their problems and needs and prays for them based on that. One of his employers was a young couple who desperately wanted to have a child but could not.

Thomas asked me to visit them and pray for them, because as Christians we believe in the power of prayer. I told Thomas that I didn't have to pray for the couple and that he could pray for them. I encouraged him by explaining that he was indeed a blessing to his host nation. I taught Thomas how to pray for his employers and to tell them about the healing power of Jesus Christ, which he did. A year later, the couple had a beautiful baby boy. They were grateful to God and Thomas, a simple migrant living in the Netherlands. It was all because a migrant had prayed for his employers, and he demonstrated the unconditional love of Christ to them.

I Will Bless Those Who Bless You

This is the most important element of the migrant's blessing. It is crucial because it involves two counterparts. One is the blessed migrant, in this case Abraham, and the others are the inhabitants of the host nation, especially the believing inhabitants. "Blessing those who bless you," is like a virtuous cycle. The native believers are blessing the migrant believers, and the migrants will in turn bless the host nation and the church. As a conference speaker and evangelist, I travel to different nations in Europe. One thing I notice, which hurts my heart, is that most of the time, there is a lack of fellowship between migrant and native churches. For instance, I met a group of female Filipino believers who with a pastor had established a church that met every Sunday in a certain nation in Europe. Now, they were growing faster than the average native church, and therefore, they were looking for a suitable building in which to worship. They contacted various native churches to rent their building for a few hours each Sunday. What were the responses?

Almost 90 percent of the native churches said, "We do not recognize you as a church but as a fellowship," and some said, "Our building is available for your fellowship if you choose to become members of our church and attend our services in the morning and in the afternoons have your fellowship."

Hidden arrogance and discrimination must be eliminated in the church. Believers from the developing world are most often victims of this once they are in another country. The situation is getting better in some nations like England or Holland, yet in others, there is still work to do. Once I traveled to an European country where there were about five hundred believers at a Christian conference. The attendees were all white. Yet when I walked in the streets of that particular town, I saw many migrants. There were people from India, Ghana, Sri Lanka, Nigeria, and many other nations. Later on, I asked the pastor in charge whether they had identified the migrant churches in that town. His response was very cold. It seemed to me that he did not want to acknowledge that there were migrants in the town who were believers and who gathered together in ghettos, in flats, in the basements of polluted garages, or in parking lots. This saddened my heart!

Blessing the migrants and fellowshipping with them blesses the church in the host nation and makes them prosper. Migrants are a very fragile group in society. It is the duty of the church to reach out and bless these migrants. If you are a Christian in a host nation, reach out to the migrants in your town. Remember the story of Jesus coming to Jerusalem and entering the temple. He was furious after He saw the merchants selling doves and other goods in the courts of the temple. He turned down the table of the moneymakers and said, "My house shall be the house of prayer for all the nations." Jesus was quoting from Isaiah 56. Why would Jesus say that? What is the connection between His anger and the prayer for the nations?

In those days, Jews traveled from various parts of the world to celebrate the Passover and the religious festivals until the day of Pentecost, but the native Jewish leaders and the religious system did not allow those migrant believers to enter some parts of the temple or the temple itself, yet they allowed money-makers to do business in the temple courts. This broke the heart of the Savior and made Him angry. Also, do not forget that on the day of Pentecost, the first men who witnessed the outpouring of the Holy Spirit upon the disciples were migrants from Persia, Arabia, and many other nations. Peter delivered his first sermon to the migrants, the same ones whom the religious system did not allow into the temple. In southeastern Amsterdam, there is a ghetto called Bijlmer. As far as I know, fifty-five various nationalities live together in the Bijlmer. People from Africa, especially from Ghana, Nigeria, are well established there. Walking the streets of Bijlmer makes you feel as though you are walking in an African nation. Just like in any other ghetto, there is crime like robberies, shootings, and killings.

Despite this fact, Bijlmer has the largest concentration of Pentecostal churches in the Netherlands and perhaps even in Western Europe. There are at least 150 churches with an average Sunday attendance of thirty to three hundred people. These churches are made up of migrants from Ghana, Nigeria, Surinam, and the Philippines. There are also some from Dutch churches. The members are migrants who came to Europe to find jobs or join a family member who was already there.

Those who speak Dutch averagely make at the most minimum wage, and not all of them have a legal residence permit to stay in Europe. Yet there is revival among them; they are in love with Jesus and trust in God. On a Friday night when I pass through the streets of this area's neighborhoods, I hear music, drums, and praying believers. Almost all of them are migrants. There are 150 churches, yet not even 10 percent of them enjoy a convenient church building. They make buildings of wood with low security systems and worship there. Recently, the situation in Bijlmer has been changing. I also had been ministering for more than five years in this kind of hard situation. On Sundays, the service smelled because of the mountain of garbage next door, or the roof leaked while I delivered my sermon. Despite the building's condition, my ministry has been able to reach eighty-five nations from a tiny, wooden, and smelly building. God is truly blessing us. While these migrant believers worship in smelly, stinky, leaking buildings, many national churches outside southeastern Amsterdam enjoy comfortable buildings.

The native churches should reach out a hand to the migrant churches and bless them with all of their ability and power to fulfill the Abrahamic promise, "whoever will bless you, I (God) will bless."

A Special Message for You

Abraham obeyed what God asked him to do: he traveled and because he lived a life of obedience and faith, everywhere he went he was blessed. If you are a migrant and are wondering why you are where you presently are, begin to examine your life. Is there any sign of rebellion? Do your best to obey what God has placed in your heart. Abraham was a migrant who easily fits in the profile of the Great Commission. Abraham had to leave his country because God asked him to do so. At the same time, Jesus Christ is calling every Christian to do something similar: "go and make disciples of all nations, baptizing them in the name of the Father and of the Son and of the Holy Spirit, and teaching them to obey everything I have commanded you. And surely I am with you always, to the very end of the age." *(Matt. 28:19)*

The secret for you to be a blessed migrant begins with sharing the gospel with the people around you, especially with those from your hosting nation. Make priorities in your migrant life. This is the foundation of Abrahamic blessing. Also, Jesus said:

> Therefore I tell you, do not worry about your life, what you will eat or drink; or about your body, what you will wear. Is not life more important than food, and the body more important than clothes? Look at the birds of the air; they do not sow or reap or store away in barns, and yet your heavenly Father feeds them. Are you not much more valuable than they? Who of you by worrying can add a single hour to his life? And why do you worry about clothes?

See how the lilies of the field grow. They do not labor or spin. Yet I tell you that not even Solomon in all his splendor was dressed like one of these. If that is how God clothes the grass of the field, which is here today and tomorrow is thrown into the fire, will he not much more clothe you, O you of little faith? So do not worry, saying, "What shall we eat?" or "What shall we drink?" or "What shall we wear?"

For the pagans run after all these things, and your heavenly Father knows that you need them. But seek first his kingdom and his righteousness, and all these things will be given to you as well. Therefore do not worry about tomorrow, for tomorrow will worry about itself. Each day has enough trouble of its own. *(Matt. 6:25-34)*

Regardless what you do or in what kind of circumstances you live: wealthy or poor, documented or undocumented, with a visa or without a visa, do your best to obey the word of God and tell to others about the unconditional love of Jesus Christ. Seek His kingdom, and He will provide for you. One time, I visited a group of undocumented migrants. They lived in a basement of an old factory building. Yet when looking at them, my heart cried of joy because they were full of love and grace; they did not worry about what they would eat, drink, or wear, and they focused their minds on the gospel. They trusted in God's Spirit. You too can be like them, by trusting in God's word and sharing God's love with others. This is your first step toward becoming a blessed migrant, like Abraham.

Blessed Migrants

Jacob, a cheating migrant

Unlike the Abraham's story, Jacob's motivation of traveling was not out of obedience to God's word but out of a lifestyle full of deception. He simply fled because he cheated his brother and his father. Jacob deceived his brother, Esau, by skillfully stealing his birthright, which was very valuable then.

The boys grew up, and Esau became a skillful hunter, a man of the open country, while Jacob was a quiet man, staying among the tents. Isaac, who had a taste for wild game, loved Esau, but Rebekah loved Jacob. Once when Jacob was cooking some stew, Esau came in from the open country, famished. He said to Jacob, "Quick, let me have some of that red stew! I'm famished!" (That is why he was also called Edom.) Jacob replied, "First sell me your birthright." "Look, I am about to die," Esau said. "What good is the birthright to me?" But Jacob said, "Swear to me first." So he swore an oath to him, selling his birthright to Jacob. Then Jacob gave Esau some bread and some lentil stew. He ate and drank, and then got up and left . . . *(Gen. 25:27–34)*

Jacob easily took advantage of his brother by taking advantage in that moment, making him swear away his birthright. Esau, on the other hand, was so weak that he couldn't endure his temporary hunger. Sometimes people get into situations in which they are weak and need instant help; therefore, they are willing to do anything to solve their problems no matter what the consequences. Don't let life's hardship force you into the manipulation of others who would take advantage of you. Jacob did the same to his own father, as is written in Genesis 27. He deceived his father, so that he made sure his father gave him the blessings intended for Esau. In those days, once someone had said the words of blessing, there was no way to take it back. That was the power of those spoken words. After cheating his father, Jacob knew that his brother was going to kill him. Jacob fled to save his own life. That was why Jacob became a migrant; he had no divine calling.

But why did God still honor Jacob, a cheating migrant? There are many reasons, but one of them is that God had an oath with Abraham, the grandfather of Jacob, and Isaac, the father of Jacob, to bless their off-spring, and God never changes His promises. No matter how many promises God has given, they will all come to pass, not because you are good and holy but because God loves you and His promise to His children never fails.

Second, Jacob knew a secret then that even contemporary Christians do not fully practice—the power of the spoken word. Why would Jacob deceive his brother and his father for just a few words of blessing? He was not after the wealth or position. Jacob deceived them because he valued the spoken word that came from his father's mouth.

He knew that once those words were spoken, there was no turning back. Jacob valued his father's verbal blessing; Esau did not take it seriously, otherwise he would not have exchanged it for a bowl of soup when he was hungry. Just like Jacob, you have to value the Father's blessing given to you through Jesus Christ. There are two types of people in the world—those who do everything to hold on to the Father's word and promises and those who exchange them for the immediate solutions.

The Story of the South and West

The story of Jacob and Esau reminds me of the story of colonization. Centuries ago, a lot of missionaries traveled to parts of the unknown world to preach the gospel to those who had never heard it. However along the way, their eyes fell on the gold, diamonds, and other resources that those territories possessed. Suddenly, the sacred call changed into a commercial call. They started buying off and exploiting the natives. And just as Esau sold his birthright, the nations in the South sold their birthrights to the Europeans.

There were chiefs in Africa who sold their African brothers to the white man to get guns. Little did they know that it was the beginning of selling Africa to others and of another evil episode of slavery in human history. The Western nations were just like Jacob, who exploited his brother for his birthright. They killed, robbed the land of its natural resources, divided up the ground, and eventually made the inhabitants their own slaves.

What Goes Around Comes Around

Jacob deceived his father, by taking advantage of his father's failing eyesight. When he arrived as a migrant in Paddan Aram and met his cousin Rachel, he fell in love with her. Rachel's father and Jacob's uncle, Laban, promised Jacob that after seven years in his service, he would allow Jacob to marry Rachel.

For seven years, Jacob served Laban with the hope to marry Rachel, but Laban cheated him, and on what was supposed to be Jacob and Rachel's wedding day, he disguised his older daughter, Leah, who had weak eyes *(Gen. 29:17)*, and wed her to Jacob. Just as Jacob abused his father's depreciated vision, he was now tricked into marrying a wife who had weak eyes. Everything that you do has consequences in life, and what goes around comes around. Today, thousands of migrants—some the sons and daughters of former slaves—are settling in the West.

Some come to evangelize, and some come for economic or political reasons, but they keep on coming. They use and sometimes even abuse the social infrastructures and benefits there. This may irritate many Westerners, but do not forget that this is because of the things that have happened centuries ago.

The Westerners were also once migrants in those nations, and sadly enough, they inflicted worse things on the natives there than some migrants are doing now in their nations. The West cannot just say that they are full, and they cannot afford to take care of more people in their nations.

When Africa or the Philippines were colonized, were their inhabitants asked? The West just did it without even thinking about the consequences. That is why if people from those nations come to you now, you have to show them hospitality. I have noticed an important fact: the Christians from those colonized nations are now immigrating to the nations that colonized them to share the life-changing message of Jesus Christ.

They are preaching the message that those nations once tried to share with them centuries ago. For example, there are many Indonesians in Holland who are having successful ministries, and they are reaching the Dutch people who once tried to bring the gospel to them but partially failed. People from Surinam fall into the same category.

There are many Surinamese churches that are reaching the Dutch, and those churches, by Dutch standards, could even be called "mega-churches." Great Britain colonized Nigeria, and today, God is using Nigerian believers to reach the British people. Japan once colonized Korea; today, there are many Korean migrants in Japan preaching the gospel to the Japanese.

Therefore, Westerners must repent for the things their forefathers did, and then they must embrace their migrant brothers and sisters and support them. The reason behind the cases of criminality and casualty among the migrants in the West is because what goes around comes around. This circle will only break if believers in the host countries love and care for migrants and are hospitable to migrant believers.

Jacob Wrestled with God

There came a time in Jacob's life when God had to deal with him to make him a better person and change him from a cheating migrant to a blessed migrant. That night Jacob got up and took his two wives, his two maidservants and his eleven sons and crossed the ford of the Jabbok. After he had sent them across the stream, he sent over all his possessions.

So Jacob was left alone, and a man wrestled with him till daybreak. When the man saw that he could not overpower him, he touched the socket of Jacob's hip so that his hip was wrenched as he wrestled with the man. Then the man said, "Let me go, for it is daybreak." But Jacob replied, "I will not let you go unless you bless me." The man asked him, "What is your name?" "Jacob," he answered. Then the man said, "Your name will no longer be Jacob, but Israel, because you have struggled with God and with men and have overcome." Jacob said, "Please tell me your name." But he replied, "Why do you ask my name?" Then he blessed him there. So Jacob called the place Peniel, saying, "It is because I saw God face to face, and yet my life was spared." The sun rose above him as he passed Peniel, and he was limping because of his hip. Therefore to this day the Israelites do not eat the tendon attached to the socket of the hip, because the socket of Jacob's hip was touched near the tendon. *(Gen. 32:22–32)*

After everybody went across the river, Jacob was alone. On that night, God wrestled with him all night. He could not overpower Jacob. No one could win. Similarly, I believe that God wrestles with all of us, but God does not want to win by force. He has given you free will, and He cannot force you when you have free will. He can wrestle with you, but He never forces people. Life is a matter of choices, and what you choose determines the direction of your life.

Nations also make choices that determine the course of their history. Along that line, Jacob realized that God was wrestling with him to change him, from a wandering migrant—Jacob—to a blessed migrant—Israel.

I believe Jacob represents the West and that God is now wrestling with the West. God wants to deal with the West and make her know that nothing she owns—the technology, science, wealth, infrastructure, or fame—can compete with God and His plans for her. As long as the West tries to win the wrestling match with God, the situation will get worse: a global increase in terrorism, war, social unrest, and ethnic tensions. If the West humbles herself and lets God bless her, just like Jacob did, then the Christ, Son of Righteousness, will heal many of the world's wounds.

Be honest with each other, remember what has happened in the past, and repent. Maybe the modern-day, high-tech generation of the West does not have enough time to remember what has happened in the past, but God remembers. He remembers the torture castles in Ghana where the slaves were held for days, weeks, and months, waiting to be exported as objects. There, the sellers humiliated, tortured, raped, and killed them just because a group of aggressive migrants wanted their land and their resources. God has never forgotten when the Spanish army, under the blessing of the priest, killed thousands of Indians in Central and South America just because the colonizers considered them pagans. I believe that roots of today's poverty are found in those dark days of the West's colonialism.

Some of the West's success is due to the bloodshed of many Africans and the unheard cries of many mothers, fathers, daughters, and sons in slavery. Also during the cold war, the West supported the Islamic countries without understanding the religion behind the regimes—they just wanted allies.

Now, the West easily labels the Muslim nations as aggressive, but she has forgotten the cruelties she did in the name of Jesus, the Bible, and the church. Could Islamic terrorism result from hundreds years of frustrations, ignorance, hatred, and anger? What should Christians in the West do? They have to pray for the migrants. They also have to serve the migrants in their nations, regardless of the migrants' religious beliefs.

They have to embrace them with love and listen to their stories before they can judge them. They have to preach the gospel to them with their actions and not just their words. Only the love of Christ can melt anger and hate into a candle of hope and love.

A Special Message for You

The story of Jacob can inspire every migrant. Even though Jacob's motivation for immigrating was not pure, in a certain moment of his life, he surrendered himself to God and repented for his sins. From then, he turned into a blessed migrant. Maybe you have had a lifestyle that resembles Jacob's life. You have had issues and problems in your past, which have caused you to be dishonest with others. It does not matter what you have done. Everyone has made mistakes; sometimes those mistakes harm you and those around you. But God can help you change your life.

All you have to do is repent and ask God for forgiveness for those things. For example, some migrants like to cheat the hosting government's welfare system, getting welfare money, and secretly working. In doing so, they earn money from both sides. Other migrants even take advantage of fellow migrants, by lending them money with high interest rate or renting rooms to those undocumented migrants for a very high price.

This is abuse. I hope and pray that none of you who are reading this book have committed such acts. If so, there is always a chance for you to repent and change. Remember that what goes around comes around. How you treat others is how one day you will be treated. Did you have arguments with your parents before you traveled? Have you been dishonest financially? Have you taken advantage of people for your own gain? Are you cheating the government of the nation hosting you? Think about it. If so, repent and God will help you change from a cheating migrant to a blessed migrant.

Blessed Migrants

Joseph, a forgiving migrant

The life of Joseph is a great example and an encouragement to millions of migrants worldwide. He was a great migrant. Joseph's journey started with two important dreams that he had when he was young. In his dreams, God revealed to him the destiny that was awaiting him. The two dreams and the special love that Jacob had for his son, Joseph, made the other brothers jealous.

One day, his father sent him to check on his brothers while they were out shepherding the flock. Joseph did not know that it was the last time he would see his father because his brothers betrayed him. As soon as his brothers saw him, they attacked him, tore his robe, threw him into the pit, and eventually sold him to some Ishmaelites, who took him as a slave to Egypt. When he entered Egypt, he was beaten and betrayed. He was emotionally and physically abused. *(Gen. 37)*

Today, there are many migrants who have left their countries because they have been betrayed by family, friends, or the political or religious leaders of their country. I have met migrants here in Europe who have experienced heavy traumas because they lost their moms, dads, or other family members in cruel and barbaric ways. Genocides in Africa have caused millions of people to seek refuge in neighboring nations. Some of them arrived in Europe with emotional baggage containing bitter memories and cruel tragedies.

What Happened in Egypt?

Later, the Ishmaelites sold Joseph to Potiphar. The Bible says that during this time, Joseph prospered. God blessed him and gave him success in everything he did. Even his master had favor on him and entrusted him with all of his properties. *(Gen. 39:3–5)*

Because Joseph was a well-built man, Potiphar's wife was attracted to him, and she wanted to sleep with him. However, Joseph continually refused. This enraged Potiphar's wife, and she accused Joseph of attempted rape. Therefore, Joseph ended up in prison. But the Bible says that even in prison God blessed him and he prospered. *(Gen. 39:20–23)*

In prison he interpreted dreams, and they all came to pass. He became a blessing even to those in prison. Pharaoh heard about a man who interpreted dreams who was imprisoned, and one day after he had a bad dream that no one could explain, he sent for Joseph. Joseph told him what it meant, and through Joseph's interpretation, he saved many Egyptians from a great famine. Pharaoh appointed him the second in command, a kind of prime minister. What a challenging life—from once a slave to a prince! One day, when drought struck Canaan, the brothers of Joseph traveled to Egypt to get food. As they entered Egypt, Joseph recognized them. After testing them, he revealed his identity to his brothers. He supported them, and so the sons of Israel; including his father, Jacob; entered Egypt, and their children remained there for almost 430 years.

A Lesson for Migrants

What can migrants learn from Joseph? How is it that a slave ended up being the second-most important man in the land? Is that also possible for modern-day migrants? I believe the greatest secret behind Joseph's success story was integrity. Even though he was a slave, he could have committed adultery with his master's wife. He could have secured his position there and found his way out of slavery. But he did not do that. He was loyal to God and to man.

Many migrants today (being a migrant, I have the right to say this) come to the host nation and start abusing the system to get ahead. They start working and go on welfare or lie to the government to stay in the land. God honors integrity and loyalty. Once you choose the honest path, God will open the gates of blessing and prosperity in the land in which you live.

Also, loyalty to his master carried him far. If you are loyal to those for whom you work, regardless of how small or big your responsibilities are, the doors of promotion will be opened. Some migrants like to cheat their bosses, and they have many excuses to justify their acts. Those people will come to a bad end. Joseph was excellent in serving his boss. Joseph was also loyal to his host nation, Egypt. Migrants must love and serve the nation in which they live as if they were in their own homeland.

If you live in a certain nation, start talking positively about it. Start to love and serve that country. Do not complain about it but be grateful. When you are a Christian migrant, you especially must bless the land in which you live. You have to pray for that nation.

When I meet some migrant believers, they complain about their host nation, "These people will never receive Christ," or "It is very hard to reach these people for Christ. They are stubborn." Do not talk like this. If you live in Holland, love Holland. If you live in the United States, love the United States. If you are in Australia, love Australia.

Another secret of Joseph's success was that he was ready to suffer for the truth. He suffered because he served his God with all of his heart and put Him and His commands as his highest priority. He knew that if he chose to do evil (give in to Potiphar's wife), he would become free and find his way out of Egypt. However, he refused and suffered for his beliefs. The path of righteousness is very hard and filled with rocks and thorns, but in the end it will lead to promotion and favor.

Joseph's Gift Brought Him Far

Despite all of the disappointment and betrayal, Joseph learned to make something out of his life. He learned to be satisfied even when he was put in prison. Also, he practiced his God-given gift and interpreted the dreams people brought to him. Blessed migrants should use their gifts, whether they are spiritual or non-spiritual. If they use them in godly ways and practice them with integrity, God will bless them and bring them into the presence of kings and the elite. Desire excellence in your work and be precise in fulfilling your tasks. This will bring you far.

Colonial Bitterness

Joseph had every reason to be bitter, disappointed, and angry. He also could have sought revenge. However, he refused. He chose forgiveness and grace. Genesis 45 describes how Joseph received his brothers, who betrayed him and sold him to Egypt. He embraced them with love and forgave them. He said to his brothers:

> But God sent me ahead of you to preserve for you a remnant on earth and save your lives by a great deliverance. So then, it was not you who sent me here, but God. He made me father to Pharaoh, lord of his entire household and ruler of all Egypt. *(Gen. 45:7-8)*

The story of Joseph reminds me of colonialism and slavery. People sold many blacks and Asians to foreign powers to be slaves. Today, the great-grandchildren of those slaves are coming back to the nations who colonized them. Some are still bitter and angry about the things that happened more than three hundred years ago. They commit crimes and have to justify it simply because they cannot forgive. However, blessed migrants should forgive and deal with the past through grace and embracing the love that was given to them through Christ. There must come a time when the blessed migrants from the Third World start praying for the nations that colonized them and forgive them. Those kinds of feelings hide racial issues both in the

United States and Europe, and only the love of Christ can bring healing to both peoples—the abused and the abusers.

A Special Message for You

Joseph's life reminds me of a migrant believer's story I heard when I was at a conference. He was living in Spain, had no proper job, and had an expiring visa. His life was full of worries; he did not know what to do or where to go. In the midst of this, he came across the previous edition of this book, Blessed Migrants.

He read the book from cover to cover, and it blessed him. As he was thinking and praying about the things he had read in this book, he came across a newspa- per ad for an IT specialist in Canada. One of the requirements was that the applicant must speak French. He prayed and asked God to give a new opportunity. He applied, and against all expectations and circumstances, he got the job. He moved to Canada, started working, and became very successful. However, eventually the company demanded that he works on Sundays.

Because this man was a Christian, he refused and unfortunately lost his job. He was kind of disappointed but found another job, not as an IT specialist but as a janitor. He sacrificed his IT job and his large salary to become a janitor. However, just like Joseph, he did his job excellently.One day, when the CEO of the company visited the building, he noticed that his company had never been so clean. He asked about it, and they told him about the man and brought him to the CEO's office. The CEO asked him, "What else can you do besides cleaning?" He replied that he was good with computers. The CEO asked the head of their computer department to check his skills and teach this blessed migrant about their computer system. Within a few hours, the person responsible for the computer department called the CEO to inform him that this man was far more advanced than they thought. Little by little, he got projects and fulfilled them with excellence. Until one day, the CEO promoted him and gave him one of the highest positions in the company.

Today, this man is traveling on a private jet of his boss all around the world doing business for that company. At the same time, he witnesses about Christ to his CEO and colleagues. Is this not wonderful? Migrants who choose loyalty and integrity can be so blessed. Whoever you are and whatever you do, do it with excellence and perform it with loyalty and integrity first to God and then to people around you.

Blessed Migrants

Ruth, a bridge-building migrant

Ruth's life is a great inspiration for every migrant. Ruth was not an Israelite; she was a Moabite married to one of the sons of Naomi, a Jew from Bethlehem. There was always tension between Israelites and Moabites. Nevertheless, Naomi had left Bethlehem for Moab because of a famine in Israel. Her sons married two Moabite women, but unfortunately some years later her sons died, leaving the two women to be widows. One of them was Ruth.

After the death of her sons, Naomi decided to go back to Bethlehem and live there because all of her family was dead. She released her daughters-in-law from all of their duties and told them to go back to their own families. One of them did, but Ruth remained with Naomi and decided to travel with her to Bethlehem. She became a migrant in Israel. Living as a non-Jew in Israel then was not easy, especially when you were from Moab. When she traveled with Naomi to Bethlehem, her life situation was not good. Her husband had passed away, and she had had a lot of sorrow.

She also was a poor migrant who had to care for her Jewish mother-in-law. When she came to Bethlehem as a migrant, she did not know the customs and culture very well. Yet, the Lord adopted her into Judah's tribe when she married Boaz, a wealthy man from Bethlehem. Boaz and Ruth became ancestors of the great King David and also Jesus Christ.

What Was Her Secret?

First of all, she, like Joseph, was a person of loyalty. She was loyal to her mother-in-law, even to the point of leaving all behind to follow her. She also accepted her mother-in-law's God, nation, and customs as her own. She built a bridge between her culture and Naomi's. If you ever want to advance the gospel in the world, you have to build bridges between nations and cultures.

I am not saying that you have to accept a culture's every element, especially if it is ungodly or unholy. My point is the same as that of the apostle Paul:

> When I am with the Jews, I become one of them so that I can bring them to Christ. When I am with those who follow the Jewish laws, I do the same, even though I am not subject to the law, so that I can bring them to Christ.
>
> When I am with the Gentiles who do not have the Jewish law, I fit in with them as much as I can. In this way, I gain their confidence and bring them to Christ. But I do not discard the law of God; I obey the law of Christ. When I am with those who are oppressed, I share their oppression so that I might bring them to Christ. Yes, I try to find common ground with everyone so that I might

bring them to Christ. I do all this to spread the Good News, and in doing so I enjoy its blessings.
(1 Cor. 9:20–23, NLT)

Ruth learned to build a bridge—of love, sacrifice, and endurance. The people of the world cannot see Jesus or feel Him. Their only path to Jesus is through encountering Him in you, fellow Christians. Christians cannot reach the world with arrogance and a superiority attitude. Building bridges means you respect and accept the people of a certain nation and culture but still remain true to the Lord. As a blessed migrant, you have to love the nation in which you live. You have to consider their nation and customs as your own. You have to serve that nation as you would your own.

As a blessed migrant living in the Netherlands, I have learned to honor this nation. I love its language, and I enjoy its people. I have made an oath before God that I will serve this country as if it were my own native land. I love its queen and pray for its cabinet and its political development. Of course, I am aware that there are ungodly things happening. Yet, I have trained myself to speak positively about the Netherlands.

Many people live for years in a certain nation and still do not speak the language properly. They do not practice the hosting land's customs properly. As a blessed migrant, you have to work within the culture's framework. You cannot go to a village somewhere in the Middle East dressed as a Western capitalist and start singing Don Moen or Vineyard songs. It will not be effective. You have to learn and respect the customs, the dress code, and the language of the nations to which you travel.

That was what Paul did. He never ignored the customs and cultures; instead, he used them to build bridges. And through that bridge, he advanced the kingdom. He knew Greek culture.

That was why when he was in a coliseum in Athens, he emphasized a monument with the inscription, "to an unknown god." He said to them that even though they had many gods, as they had written, there was an unknown god, and he came to speak about that God, the God of heaven and Earth. That God was no longer unknown; He had revealed Himself through the being of Jesus Christ. How could Paul have done that if he had not known the Greek language and culture well?

Finally, Ruth stayed humble. She was very hungry and poor when she arrived in Bethlehem with her ill mother-in-law. She went to Boaz's grain field, started gathering leftover grain, and brought it to Naomi. Boaz noticed that, and he gave her favor to take as much as she wanted. Later on, they fell in love, and Ruth married Boaz, the wealthiest man in town. Never despise small beginnings. It is in the small things that God is testing you. Many people want to be successful in a short period of time. Godly success, though, begins in small things, and it develops slowly!

Fast success is dangerous and destructive. Many migrants want to be successful instantaneously, and they make bad decisions to be successful quickly. They end up in dealing drugs or committing financial fraud until they are arrested and deported back to their country. I remember the day that I arrived in the Netherlands. As a migrant who had traveled through the mountains in freezing cold temperatures, in which a baby had even died, it had been a terrible journey. I arrived in Europe without anything—only bags with a few clothes. My parents and I, with my sisters, started life at ground zero. I remember when I went to school, I had to learn the language and participate in normal school. It was one of the most awful times of my life. I know that my parents did not have money. We could not buy clothes or shoes. As a teenager, I went to the garbage cabins of the neighborhood at night and opened the bags, trying to find shoes, clothes, or other things.

Whenever my mom asked me how I had gotten those things, I told her that my friends at school had given them to me. In college, I worked late at the post office, sometimes from midnight until 6:00 AM. From there, I went right to the university. I have seen many difficult things, but I have learned to be faithful and grateful through it all.

Thank God that today, I am a successful and blessed person living in Europe. And because it was during this journey that I gave my life to Jesus Christ, things started to change in a better way. I am blessed by serving the King of Glory and by sharing my experience with thousands of migrants in Europe and around the globe. Like me, Ruth dedicated her life to God and His commandments, and He guided her to the fields that belonged to Boaz. Later, she sat at a table with him and dipped bread in wine with him. Ruth received favor from Boaz, and he blessed her. Boaz was her kinsman redeemer, someone who supports and redeems the poor and oppressed in his family. He even helps those in his extended family. Eventually, Ruth married Boaz, and he gave her what she wanted: a husband, a family, and a place to call home.

A Special Message for You

What is your story? Did you lose a precious one in your life? Have you experienced a recent tragedy? It is time to start a new life. As a migrant, begin to hope in a better future. Because you are in a foreign country, just like Ruth, learn the customs, the language, and culture of that nation. I often ask many people who have complained about discrimination and rejection in their adopted society, "Do you speak the language properly? What do you know about the country in which you are living? How much do you care about the country and its people?"

Often they fall silent before answering me. Remember, even the hardest man or woman in the society who is against migrants will notice your passion and love for their country and their language. I assure you that once they see that, they will begin to like you and eventually love you. If you want people to open the doors of opportunities for you, and if you want the love and respect of people in your host nation, begin to respect them and love them by making their culture your own and their language a part of your life. Respect is earned and not gained. Those simple things will bring you far because they build bridges that bring people together.

Daniel a courageous migrant

When Daniel was young, he was a member of the royal household in the kingdom of Judah. After the Babylonians attacked Judah, Daniel witnessed a cruel war, and he probably experienced some form of trauma from watching them destroy his homeland.

The Babylonians separated him from his parents and took him back to their land. Daniel entered Babylon as a hostage and ended up at the king's palace. Soon after, the Persians defeated Babylon, and Daniel became a high-ranking official under the king of Persia. Later, he became the most important person in Persia after the king. And through him, people glorified the name of God throughout the Persian Empire and blessed Daniel's countrymen, the Jews, in Persia. God blessed Daniel because he was not ashamed of his God and the laws of his faith. In Daniel 1,

Daniel refused to defile himself with food from the royal table. Instead, he chose to eat vegetables. Yet after eating vegetables for ten days, he looked far better and healthier than those who had defiled themselves with unclean food. Daniel also had the courage to say, "No," and refuse. Daniel refused to pray to King Darius after a decree that for thirty days everyone who did not pray to the king would be put to death. Therefore, the king sentenced Daniel to death and had him thrown into a den of Persian lions.

Yet, the lions did not harm him, and he came out alive. The king promoted him to a higher rank, and he received more esteem in the royal palace. Many migrants defile themselves with the unholy customs and manners of their hosting culture. Instead of picking up the right elements and using them carefully, they choose the things that destroy them. I remember friends of mine with whom I studied the language and went to school.

As soon as the weekends arrived, my friends, who were also migrants, went to discos, drank alcohol, and used drugs. Yet, remained home and studied hard. Almost all of them did not enter a university, finish school, or get a good job. Many of them ended up being jobless and living in an insecure environment. I graduated from the university and converted to Christianity. Many years later, I got married and had two sons and a beautiful daughter. The Holy Spirit helped me to build a ministry that impacted many people from at least eighty-five nations around the world.

Many people lose themselves as soon as they are in a different environment and country. Just like Daniel, I have learned to hold the cup of the king of this world and yet not bow to him. Why should I apologize for my values and belief in God? Many Christians are very timid and too shy to express their faith in their daily life. I have never understood how someone can pick up his cigarette pack, light a match, and smoke in my presence without asking permission, and yet I should be ashamed of practicing my faith in the world. If he can have that kind of boldness, why should not I have the same when celebrating my God?

I see some young couples in the busy streets of Amsterdam kissing each other intensely as everyone passes by, and yet the same people ridicule a pastor preaching a message in the same street. The world is not ashamed of the products it produces, advertises, and sells. It advertises cigarettes in such a tempting way that it makes you feel like smoking, and the producers are not even ashamed of the millions of former smoking cancer patients diagnosed yearly or of creating broken families and homes after fires that started by cigarettes. The world brings the most ugly and terrible things right into your living rooms and teaches your kids things they should not know.

The world is not ashamed of producing a society full of rape, rage, criminality, rebellion, racism, and sensationalism. The world is terribly deceived and is continuing that deception. For the world, everything evil is now tolerated, and everything based on the word of the living God is considered old-fashioned—démodé.

This is how the world functions; it changes the basic God-given values of life and justifies those changes by tagging it as modern and humane. However, I am not ashamed of practicing my faith in the world just like the world is not ashamed of its own. The world sells confusion, death, and destruction, and my faith offers life and righteousness.

Who should really be ashamed?

These days the majority of youth are having sex even before they have reached the age of fourteen because society says that having no sex before eighteen is considered strange by their peers. Youth are exposed to television shows and movies that pollute their innocent minds. Advertisers design promotions in such a way that there must be a naked woman in them to sell things that people do not need.

Some Christians are ashamed to mention that they are virgins for fear of being ridiculed. Remember, it's not cool to sell your body to a moment of passion that may leave you with lifelong consequences. It's cool to refuse your body to a person who is not your wife or husband. It is good to not let others take advantage of your body and then leave you with a child or a disease. Our world is getting worse.

Today, youth between the ages of sixteen and twenty-five are smoking, drinking, and partying. Smoking a cigarette alone does not satisfy the soul anymore, so they use drugs to get high. Now if someone—a teenager or adult—does not do those things, he or she may be considered weird. Take the workplace, for instance. In Japan if you do not go out, drink with your colleagues, or frequently visit strip clubs, then something is supposedly wrong with you. *(Lee 2008)*

Two thousand years ago, the Roman Caesars persecuted Christians. The Christians came with the message that Jesus was King and God. The Caesars did not like this statement, so one of the Caesars, Nero, declared that from then on he was God and King, and everyone must bow before him. He also gave people the chance to bow before him. If they did not bow, they had to die. The sign for not bowing before the

Caesar was the fish. Christians placed this sign on their doors, declared that they would not bow, and were fed to lions and snakes in arenas of the Roman Empire. God is looking for believers who will not bow before the world, the Caesar of this time. He is looking for those who choose not to be ashamed of the gospel of Christ. This is the measure of an excellent Christian life.

A Special Message for You

Maybe you are where you are now because you are a refugee, a victim of war or economic/environmental crisis. Maybe you are a modern-day Daniel. Learn to be loyal to your principles. Do not fear other people and learn to say, "No."

Many times in my life, I had great opportunities of doing things to be well-known or rich. I, however, said, "No," to them, and that proved my integrity to the principles in which I believe. This even offered me more opportunity and promotion than I would have had if I had accepted them. Once, I traveled to a certain country to speak to a group of migrant women who were domestic workers. I noticed that they were over fatigued, stressed, and unhealthy.

As I talked to them, they shared their hearts with me and told me that they were working for three or four families, cleaning their houses, babysitting, and doing their laundry even though their contract was only for one family. Often they were harshly treated, and some were even physically confronted. It happened because those precious women did not learn to say, "No." I realized that I had to preach more than an evangelistic message to them, but I had to teach them how to stand up for their values and rights. After regularly returning to that country, there is success.

Employers are beginning to change. One family has even repented for what they did to their domestic girl, and now they support her in all aspects. Learn to say, "No." People treat you how you allow them to treat you. Migrants are usually afraid to say, "No," especially when they are new in a country. Do not be like that. Be bold, honest, and sincere in your life as a migrant! Nothing is better than being yourself, believing in your values, and trusting in God. This will bring you far.

Part Two

Migrants Today

Blessed Migrants

Migrants and World Evangelization

Through the Great Commission, Jesus encouraged the disciples to become migrants, "Therefore go and make disciples of all nations, baptizing them in the name of the Father and of the Son and of the Holy Spirit, and teaching them to obey everything I have commanded you. And surely I am with you always, to the very end of the age". *(Matt. 28:19-20)*

The apostles traveled from city to city and nation to nation to fulfill what Christians call the Great Commission. From that time until when man journeyed across the oceans and through the skies, the gospel has been preached. As you read history, you can see the hand of God. Humans have made a lot of mistakes, and yet God never stopped directing all according to His divine plan.

For example, God allowed the Europeans to go to other nations and continents, not because God wanted them to colonize those nations and abuse those nations' resources but because God wanted them to evangelize the unknown nations and cultures. It was not God who encouraged colonialism and slavery. It was evil in the hearts of men, the greed, which led them to commit such cruel acts. Nevertheless, God still directs and redirects all of the scenarios toward His great plan.

Language is one example: in Africa, there are thousands upon thousands of languages and dialects. Yet today, Africans speak English, French, Portuguese, Italian and Arabic. Latin Americans are speaking Spanish, Portuguese, French, and English. Far East Asians speak English and some French. Middle Easterners speak French, English, and Arabic.

Now, the ex-colonized nations are coming back to the nations that once colonized them. Some come out of poverty and hunger, some go for education, some come because of war, but some go to preach the gospel that Europeans once tried to preach to them, but somehow failed. I believe with all of my heart that God is going to use migrants to revive Europe, North America, Far East Asia, and the Pacific nations, like Australia and New Zealand.

The statistics show that Pentecostal/Charismatic movement is the fastest-growing Christian form of faith in the world; the majority of those believers are in the developing world. There are 104 million migrants who live in rich nations. Migrants are very important for the kingdom. Remember today, the greatest nation, the United States, is the biggest exporter of the gospel in the world and a migrant nation. *(Anderson 2004)*

The first people who witnessed the Pentecost in Acts were migrants from different parts of the world. Second, the great Pentecostal movement started in a migrant church with African American minorities at Azusa Street

312 under the leadership of William Seymour, 1870–1922, the son of freed slaves. It is wonderful that the Holy Spirit visited a church of slaves' offspring.

Seymour had rented an old storage building on Azusa Street that had been a former Methodist Episcopal church. With sawdust-sprinkled floors and rough planks as benches, the daily meetings commenced at about 10 AM and went on until nighttime. The Holy Spirit visited them, and spontaneously, they began to speak and sing in tongues. It was through the Pentecostal movement that the wall between black and white in the church started to break down and women started to have more freedom in ministry.

The first white Pentecostal pastors were baptized in the Holy Spirit at the church on Azusa Street. Later in 1907, they traveled to India and brought the message of Pentecost to Calcutta. Soon Azusa Street received international attention, and the revival of Pentecost started to spread all over the United States, Latin America, Europe, Africa, and Asia. In less than two years, Azusa Street had reached twenty-five nations, like India, China, Japan, Angola, South Africa, and more.

God used the least of all, a migrant church and a storage building without beauty and visited them and displayed His glory. What was God doing? What was His plan? Why would He visit an ex-slave's son and his church? I believe God wants the migrant church to be taken seriously in the world. Christians, especially, should be more active by showing God's love and care for migrants, maybe even gaining their hearts to save their souls and giving birth to great men and women of

God. While I was living an ungodly life as a migrant, a Korean missionary, Philip, witnessed to me. He never could imagine that one day my ministry would amazingly expand to eighty-five nations worldwide.

In the coming chapters, I will share about some migrant-exporting nations as case studies, and we will try to discover God's plan for those nations and how God is using them to reach the more developed countries for Christ. In some cases, I will go even deeper and describe some individual case studies from migrants in those nations.

The Filipino Migrants

If there is any nation I admire and respect, it is the Philippines. My adoration especially goes to the millions of Filipino mothers, sisters, and daughters who are working abroad—normally doing domestic work to care for their families and indirectly blessing their nation's economy. It breaks my heart when I see those beautiful ones mistreated and underestimated just because they look small in stature.

In reality, their hearts are very big. The Philippines has gone through the valleys and shadows of death. During her history, she has been attacked and colonized by many foreign powers. The Spanish, Americans, and Japanese have played important roles in its history. Spain introduced Catholicism to the Philippines, and Americans introduced the American lifestyle and English language. The Philippines is not an economically strong nation; there are many poor people living there. They try to survive.

In Manila, there are millions of poor people throughout the city. Many in the rural areas try to find success in Manila, which makes things worse. Many Filipinos also try to find jobs abroad and in foreign countries.

As a result, the Philippines is the biggest exporter of manpower, even surpassing Pakistan, India, and China. It is estimated that 700,000 departures occur annually. Today, there are 11 million Filipinos working in 181 countries around the world. This means that 11 percent of the Filipino population is living abroad. Out of that 11 million, an estimated 546,701 Filipinos live in seven major Western European countries:

France -	47,745
Germany -	53,995
Great Britain -	200,000
Italy -	200,000
Spain -	26,505
The Netherlands -	18,456
Total -	**546,701**

Source: Wikipedia

There are 4 million Filipino workers in the United States and 2 million in Saudi Arabia. It has been my privilege and honor to work with overseas Filipino workers in my ministry, not only in Holland but also worldwide.

Unfortunately, I have noticed that many of them, especially the women, are suffering. They are well-educated people who speak English, yet they have become workers in a foreign land with low salaries. They deserve more than that.

In some countries in the Middle East, the conditions are even worse due to strongly fundamentalist Muslim laws. Even though the Philippines is pre-dominantly Catholic,

Pentecostalism is the fastest-growing Christian group. *(Pew Research Center 2006)*

Something more also happens when Filipinos go abroad. They become zealous for God, are active in evangelism, and care for their countrymen there. I have deliberately chosen this nation as an example because I truly believe that God has anointed the Filipino migrants to bring the message of love and the gospel of Christ to the nations in which they work. I will explain the stories of some Filipino domestic workers who made an impact on many people's lives. Also, I will share with you some heart-aching stories about great men and women who were martyred or tortured for Christ.

Filipinos: The God-chosen Migrants

Only narrow-minded people look at the Filipinos as little Asians, basically short and dark-skinned women and men working low-profile work. This is a big mistake.

Those people do not look beyond the short postures of my Filipino brothers and sisters to see a great people, whom God chose and sent. They are the living Daniels, Mordecais, Esthers, and servants of Naaman. Many of those Filipino migrants are God's chosen instruments to witness to the nations that host them. You have to respect, love, and help them.

Did you know that in some European nations, there are more Filipino Christian fellowships than ones of the host nation? For instance, in Orthodox Cyprus, there are about three thousand Born Again Christians. However, this number does not include the number of Filipino, Indian, Sri Lankan, and African believers. I estimate that those groups have as many Born Again Christians in Cyprus as the Cypriots have. I also know that the Filipino churches and fellowships are one of the fastest-growing churches in Cyprus. They gather in apartments, flats, and homes, where on Sundays they are turned into churches or fellowships.

Naaman's Servant's Anointing

> The king of Aram had great admiration for Naaman, the commander of his army, because through him the LORD had given Aram great victories. But though Naaman was a mighty warrior, he suffered from leprosy. At this time Aramean raiders had invaded the land of Israel, and among their captives was a young girl who had been given to Naaman's wife as a maid.
>
> One day the girl said to her mistress, "I wish my master would go to see the prophet in Samaria. He would heal him of his leprosy." So Naaman told the king what the young girl from Israel had said. "Go and visit the prophet," the king told him. "I will send a letter of introduction for you to carry to the king of Israel." So Naaman started out, taking as gifts 750 pounds of silver, 150 pounds of gold, and ten sets of clothing. The letter to the king of Israel said, "With this letter I present my servant Naaman.
>
> I want you to heal him of his leprosy." When the king of Israel read the letter, he tore his clothes in dismay and said, "This man sends me a leper

to heal! Am I God, that I can give life and take it away? I can see that he's just trying to pick a fight with me." But when Elisha, the man of God, heard that the king of Israel had torn his clothes in dismay, he sent this message to him:

"Why are you so upset? Send Naaman to me, and he will learn that there is a true prophet here in Israel." So Naaman went with his horses and chariots and waited at the door of Elisha's house. But Elisha sent a messenger out to him with this message: "Go and wash yourself seven times in the Jordan River. Then your skin will be restored, and you will be healed of leprosy."
(2 Kings 5:1–10, NLT)

After much hesitation and anger, Naaman eventuallydid what Elisha had advised him to do, and he was fully healed, went back to his country, and glorified Jehovah, the God of Israel. Naaman's servant reminds me of the millions of Filipino domestic workers in the Middle East, Asia, and Europe. Naaman's maidservant was just a worker, a slave girl taken from war, but she had the answer to the problem of the mightiest general in town. The world has leprosy, and only Christ can heal it.

The Filipinos and other migrants are telling their employers, bosses, neighbors, and colleagues that only Jesus can heal them when they surrender and wash themselves in the living water, the Holy Spirit. This was what the maidservant did for Naaman.

As I mentioned earlier, there are also 546,701 Filipino workers in Western Europe. Three important Catholic countries, Spain, France, and Italy (I do not have the figures on Portugal), hold 274,250 Filipinos; there are 200,000 in Italy alone. According to Operation World, 27.5 percent of the Philippine population is Charismatic, Pentecostal, or Evangelical. *(Johnstone and Mandrijk 2001)*

Assume this 27.5 percent of the 274,250 Filipinos who live in these three countries are active Christians (75,419). Assume they each work for one family made of three members. This means that they can reach at least 226,257 (75,419 × 3 = 226,257) people for evangelism in Spain, France, and Italy every day. Every day, 226,257 people in Spain, France, and Italy are directly or indirectly being witnessed by the Filipino population.

However, many native churches in those nations do not even recognize the Filipino churches. Some even ignore working and fellowshipping with them. In some countries, the relationship between Filipino fellowships and native churches is very limited. I think this could be because women lead the majority of the Filipino fellowships or churches; therefore, many native churches do not take them seriously. Once I was speaking with a pastor in a Western European country. He had a big church by European standards. I asked him about the Filipinos in his community. Pride and arrogance filled his comments. He considered them second-class citizens even in the kingdom, and he spoke lowly of them. He did not know that God would not be pleased with his answer; he did not know that God promised that whoever blesses Abraham and his offspring will in return be blessed; he did not know that the Filipino believers are blessed servants of God. As long as there are hidden prejudices against certain groups of people, God will not move in your lives and churches, and this hinders revival in your lands.

Cyprus, a Filipino Revival

The Lord used a Filipino domestic worker, a mother who had not seen her kids for a couple of years, to begin one of the most exciting and important revivals in Cyprus, which is still continuing today. In 1996,

God spoke to my heart to send a personal message to a Filipino sister, whom I had never met. This lady, Mama Lynn, is the sister of one of my team members in Amsterdam. Mama Lynn, however, was not an active Christian. She was going through some emotional and physical problems. The Holy Spirit urged me to reach out to her through a personal message recorded on a tape. I did, but I had no idea that it was the starting point of something much bigger.

Mama Lynn listened to the cassette, and as she heard my voice, she rededicated her life to Jesus Christ. Her life changed; joy returned to her, and she duplicated this tape and gave it to other Filipino women who were also working in Cyprus. Eight of them listened to the tape, and the same thing happened to them.

A few months later, I got a phone call from Cyprus, and those wonderful newly converted sisters invited me to come there to baptize them. It was my first visit and the start of my ministry there. Some Christians, even some Filipino churches, did not approve of my trip to Cyprus. They criticized me for going there. I went every year just for those eight sisters. However, those sisters were so filled with God's love that they could not wait. They went out to the parks and streets and witnessed to Filipinos and other Cypriots. Soon after, they finished their contract in Cyprus and returned to the Philippines. One of them was Sister Lucy. As soon as she returned to her hometown, she pioneered a Christian fellowship where there were not many Born Again churches.

Today, through her and some pastors connected to her, there are four churches. Meanwhile, in Cyprus, I still traveled there annually, and I probably gathered twenty or twenty-five Filipinos together. On one trip, I met a twenty-year-old man named Carlos who had just become a Born Again Christian. I knew he would have a key role for evangelizing Filipinos in Cyprus. I trained him and made him the leader of a small fellowship of ten to twelve people. He grew in the Spirit and in his leadership ability. Carlos and his team started praying for a greater revival in Cyprus.

Soon after, about nine Filipino fellowships united for the revival. When I went there in 1999, about 250 people filled the hall of a hotel, which encouraged the believers. The number of Filipino fellowships in the revival grew to twenty. In 2003, a whole theater—almost five hundred people, which is a huge number for Cyprus—was filled with wonderful Filipino sisters and believers from Cyprus, Nigeria, Ghana, and Egypt. They all sat together.

One Cypriot pastor told me that he was so ashamed that he never believed in the capacity of these wonderful Filipino women on fire for God. He never thought they could do this and gather so many together. All of this started with a domestic worker, a simple and lovely person who gave her life to Christ.

Christian history will remember her name in the generations to come. Today, there are many unknown migrant heroes for Christ. Maybe no one remembers their names, but God remembers. If you are a Christian and you have migrant neighbors, never underestimate them. You never know. One day, thatperson may be a catalyst for revival in your nation.

Migrant Martyrs

Filipino migrants are also impacting the Muslim world, especially Saudi Arabia, which is the birthplace of Islam. You may have heard the story of a Christian brother in Saudi Arabia named Brother Rene Camahort. Rene was a migrant worker in Saudi Arabia. In the Philippines, he worked in a brigade for a few days without sleeping. He left for Saudi Arabia and became a representative of a Saudi travel agency.

He was imprisoned for more than four years, and in 1999, the government set him free. During those years, he secretly wrote letters, which Open Doors published, of how his Filipino brothers and sisters in the Saudi prisons were tortured and even martyred. In Saudi Arabia, many employers can take advantage of their workers without being punished. The migrant workers were treated as slaves. There was a Filipino woman whose boss raped and often abused her. When she refused him, he accused her of stealing. She almost lost her arm, which was the penalty for theft according to Islamic law. Sometimes the employers do not even pay the proper salary to themigrant workers. The majority of those workers do heavy labor. Rene's job was good.

However, it did not pay well because he did not receive the wages he deserved. According to Rene, his troubles began when he complained about his salary. His boss had promised him commissions, bonuses, yearly holidays, etc. After a while, he was asked to do things for the company beyond his job description.

They asked him to fix things in the office and clean it when he was a representative of the travel agency. Because of his persistent concern about his salary, his boss accused him of fraud, and he ended up in department number four of Malaz Prison. There were one hundred Filipinos there. In department number 4, some Filipinos met regularly for Bible studies. During those studies, Rene found Christ. In bondage, he found freedom. In his letters, Rene wrote how they secretly prayed and read the Bible without being noticed by the guards or other inmates. Gradually, Christian prisoners started to respect him, and he became a good friend with Ruel, the leader of the Bible study group.

One day, early in the morning, the prison guards came and took Ruel and some other friends with them to be beheaded. Ruel, a Filipino brother, was martyred for Christ because of his faith. This is only one of thousands of stories about wonderful migrants, not just from the Philippines but also from India, Bangladesh, and Africa, whom God has used in the most hostile places in the world. How many of these migrant heroes have been killed in silence? Who cares for these great people who are ready to be martyred for their faith?

In the West, even some Christians are making Hollywood of church, and they make a lot of noise in the world and commercialize the faith. But there are millions of migrants, who are evangelizing and secretly suffering for Jesus, just like Rene and his friends.

The African Migrants

On that day I will purify the lips of all people, so that everyone will be able to worship the LORD together. My scattered people who live beyond the rivers of Ethiopia will come to present their offerings. And then you will no longer need to be ashamed of yourselves, for you will no longer be rebels against me. I will remove all the proud and arrogant people from among you. There will be no pride on my holy mountain.
(Zeph. 3:9–11, NLT)

A few verses prophesied by Zephaniah summarize the story of Africa. Zephaniah knew already that the people who lived beyond the rivers of Ethiopia would be scattered. This is the African Diaspora through slavery. Those scattered people were taken to the other side of the world as slaves, yet the Lord promised that they would come, bring offerings, and worship the Lord together.

What does it mean that people will worship together?

Does it mean that blacks and whites or the ex-slaves' sons and daughters will worship with the ex-slaveholders' children? Could it be referring to the Azusa Pentecost revival, which opened the doors for racial mixing in the church? Everyone may have different opinions on this, but one thing is sure: there is revival in Africa, especially in certain regions an nations, like Nigeria, Ghana, or South Africa. After last century's independence of African nations and increasing economical poverty, many decided to travel to Europe and the United States. In the late 1980s and 1990s, those African groups started to grow in Europe and North America.

Even today, Africans are in countries in Far East Asia, like Japan and Korea. The majority of those Africans are very spiritual Christians, who are open to the Holy Spirit. They have their own ways of praising and worshipping the Lord with rhythmic songs and a lot of dancing. Once, I was in Japan at a church in downtown Tokyo. Nigerians, Ghanaians, Filipinos, and some Japanese filled the church. This church was bigger than the average Japanese church. I traveled to Korea, saw many Africans, and heard that there were Ghanaian churches there, but very few native Korean churches were aware of their existence.

God is using Africans in Europe to advance the gospel. In England, one of the fastest growing churches is the African church, where they are reaching not only Africans but also whites and other ethnic groups. Ghanaians, Nigerians, Kenyans, Zimbabweans, and Zambians are also very active there.

France is also an interesting study: if you walk in some neighborhoods in Paris, you will come across various ads, proclaiming the kingdom of God or inviting the people to attend to a Holy Spirit miracle service. French-speaking Africans, mostly from ex-colonized nations in black Africa, organize those meetings.

Southeastern Amsterdam, a Small Africa

Earlier in this book, I discussed Bijlmer in southeastern Amsterdam. Walking through her streets feels like you are walking in an African country. The markets and shops remind me of South Africa. I call this part of Amsterdam "a small Africa." Every Sunday, when you look through your window, you see well-dressed African men and women rushing to church with Bibles in their hands. In this very small part of Amsterdam, there are about 150 churches or fellow- ships. Besides Africans, there are other ethnic groups, such as the Antilleans and Surinamese. Muslim minorities are also there. After the Surinamese, Ghanaians and Nigerians are the largest group in that region.

There are at least six thousand Ghanaians registered in the Netherlands and probably a few thousand are illegal. The majority of the Ghanaians live in Bijlmer, and many Ghanaian pastors lead big ministries. Also, Nigerians are leading churches but are more spread throughout the land. Through the African churches in Holland, even some traditional Dutch churches or old evangelical churches are undergoing revival, and so there are white churches being exposed to African ways of wor- ship and praise. My own church started in Bijlmer, and as we grew, we moved to a business district outside of that section of town. We were the first church who used a business building as a worship place. Soon after, many other churches followed to the predominantly white area. Today, in one little business district, there are at least ten to fifteen churches. The authorities are talking about calling it Christ Street or Jesus Valley. All of those churches that have moved there are African churches, which has changed the whole area's demeanor.

The fastest-growing Christian churches in Bijlmer are the Pentecostal/Charismatic churches led by Africans. However, those churches worship God in very difficult circumstances, and their members are not all rich. Some even have no proper papers to stay in Holland. Many live in little rooms in someone else's house, working hard and earning just three hundred dollars as their wage. Yet, many have learned to survive and depend upon the Lord and His promises.

I believe that my beloved African brothers are just like Joseph, yet God is going to bring them to the top and use them to reach Europeans and Americans for Jesus. They are so special. Even in the most inhumane and difficult circumstances of life in Europe, many of them still worship God with joy and happiness. Perhaps in Christ, they have learned to be content in all things.

Nigerians

Nigerians are very zealous for God and His kingdom. I believe that the Nigerians will play an increasing role in twenty-first century Christianity. Once I was eating with some of my very good Nigerian pastor friends, and they told me who or what the Nigerian Christian believers consider their primary export product.

They said: The Japanese have Toyota, the Koreans have Samsung, the Americans have General Motors, and we have the gospel. That shows how passionate and zealous Nigerians are in preaching the gospel and reaching nations for Christ. The Redeemed Church is one example of how the Nigerians penetrate the entire world, starting within their own country, then to other African countries, and finally to the rest of the world.

A friend of mine who belongs to that church once said that their motto is "five minutes from home." I did not understand what he meant, so I asked him to explain. What he meant was they wanted to establish churches all around the world so that it would only take people five minutes to walk from their homes to reach a church. Can you imagine how many churches they then have to establish? They are already doing it in Nigeria, he informed me.

Recently, I conducted a conference in the Laguna area of the Philippines. I have been traveling to that region for the past ten years and have never expected that I would see a Nigerian there. On that trip, I met a Nigerian missionary doing the work of God and evangelizing Filipinos. The Africans and, in particular, the Nigerians, are introducing to the West a different type of worship and praise by adding dancing to it.

They believe that dancing is for God. As they sing or praise or when they take an offering to God, they dance. They do not simply throw the coins in the buckets, but they dance and cheerfully give to God.

This type of worship is now becoming common, even among some European churches. A day will come when many churches, Western or non-Western, will sing worship songs, praise songs, and musical pieces that have originated from Africa, especially from Nigeria. I already have some friends who are Korean and Filipino pastors and are translating some English African songs from Nigerian/African churches into Korean and the Filipino languages.

Lastly, by choosing Nigeria as a case study in this book, it is not my intention to exclude other African nations that are active in preaching the gospel, such as Ghana, Kenya, South Africa, the French and Portuguese-speaking African nations—all of them are partaking in worldwide evangelization.

Africans have personally blessed me with their love and encouragement. I have always enjoyed worshipping and ministering to and with them.

When I was a young lad and not yet a believer, an African friend in my class, George from Ghana, shared the gospel with me. I often used to ridicule him, but today, I am grateful that he witnessed to me.

Even though I did not become a Christian right away, an African planted a seed in my heart when I was fourteen. In those days as a young boy, I dreamed of going to Africa to work there.

Now, I am blessed by many Africans in my life. I eat with them, drink with them, and sometimes wear their traditional clothes.

As a young boy, I used to write poems, and this is what I wrote many years ago:

> Africa is in my heart.
> Asia is in my blood.
> White is my color.
> Black is my pride!

The Korean Migrants

Koreans with their persistence, hard work, and courage are one of the migrant-exporting nations of the world. From the remotest areas in Africa, Latin America, and Far East Asia to Germany, France, and the United States, you can find Koreans.

In the Ukraine, I have met Ukrainian Koreans who had lived there for generations; they ate Korean food like improvised kimchi (a Korean vegetable salad) and spoke Korean. Also, in northeastern China, there are Chinese Koreans. In Central Asia, Uzbekistan, Tajikistan, and Kazakhstan there are native Koreans. In Japan alone, there are more than six hundred thousand Koreans. The majority of them were born and raised in Japan. Japan's colonization of Korea brought many of them there, and the cruelties inflicted on the Korean people throughout the history, especially recently, are unforgettable. They have been systematically massacred; the Japanese military forces have brutally and massively abused Korean women. *(Lee 2008)*

Christianity in Korea is relatively young. During the last hundred years, Korea has experienced a rapid Christianization. Today, a little more than 30 percent of

Korean people are Christians. *(Johnstone and Mandrijk 2001)*

When driving through any South Korean town, I have noticed many crosses on the buildings on the streets. Sometimes you can find a church every five hundred meters. The largest Full Gospel Church, with almost one million members each Sunday, is Yoido Full Gospel Church in South Korea, which was started by Dr. David Cho in the 1950s. *(www.fgtv.com)*

According to the statistics, South Korea sends more missionaries than any country but the United States. *(Moll 2006)* There are two ways in which the Koreans share the gospel and plant churches. The first is the classic way to send missionaries, sponsored by South Korean churches, to other nations. Korean missionaries are now almost in every part of the globe: Africa, Asia, the Middle East, former Communist nations, and South and Central America.

I admire the zeal and passion that the Koreans have for the gospel, even though they don't know the language or culture of the nations to which they are sent. For instance, millions of Koreans showered the former Soviet Union with prayers, and after the fall of communism, Korean Christians invested vast amount of money, resources, and manpower to reach those nations with the gospel.

Korean missionaries are now reaching out to the Muslim world. I personally know Koreans who have sold their houses and property to give to mission projects or sponsor worldwide mission work. I gave my life to Jesus Christ through the efforts and prayers of the

Korean people, and Koreans have always sponsored my personal ministry.

Another way in which the Koreans promote the kingdom of God is through the marketplace. There are Koreans living in Canada, the United States, Australia, the developed countries of Europe, and so forth to work. They are businessmen, shop owners, restaurateurs, or employees for major Korean companies abroad, not to mention their involvement in education and academic circles. They are often Christians.

They find each other in the foreign countries and start Korean communities and churches. Many times they affiliate with main churches back home to get a suitable pastor for their church or community. I call those Koreans who live in the Western, or modern world, marketplace Christians. Through their services in business, labor, or various sectors of the society, they practicetheir Christian faith. I know of Korean Christian medical doctors who not only treat their patients with modern medical systems, but also pray for their patients and offer them the gospel of Jesus Christ. In Germany, for instance, Korean Christians are doing a marvelous job, creating communities of faith. Those Koreans entered Germany as nurses in the 1960s and 1970s and remained in Germany to build up their lives there.

Now, there is a huge community of Koreans in Germany, and they evangelize their fellow Koreans and establish Korean churches. Those churches play an important role in encouraging local German churches that are often not growing or growing very slowly. I have a Korean pastor friend who lives in Germany and does a great job of working as a bridge between the Korean and German evangelical churches. Once in a while, they do combined gospel festivals, where they take German youth groups to Korea to sing German gospel music in the streets, at churches, and in the communities. This motivates and inspires the German believers. Then, the Koreans will do public praise, worship, and dancing exhibitions in Germany. In other words, they exchange information, inspiration, and passion with each other, so that even the mayor of this particular city in Germany welcomes those Korean Christians and offers for them to use the city facilities for their events and festivals.

Koreans in Japan

There are approximately six hundred thousand North and South Koreans in Japan today. The majority of them were born and raised in Japan. They are the third-and even fourth-generation migrants because Japanese nationality is based on lineage, and so those Korean descendants are not automatically awarded the citizenship. Once you are a Korean, you are forever a Korean. (This is very hard to understand in the West, where a third- or fourth-generation African in Europe or the United States is automatically a citizen and obtains nationality.)

There are some Koreans who have been naturalized, and some children of Korean-Japanese intermarriages have become Japanese nationals, too. Almost 1 percent of the 120 million people in Japan are either North or South Korean nationals or Japanese nationals of Korean descent. *(Lee 2008)*

After the annexation of Korea in 1910, Imperial Japan forced Koreans to become their subjects. The occupying colonial policy imposed severe control on Korea. Between the 1920s and 1930s, Japan used Korean soil for rice production to export to Japan. This caused severe famine and poverty in Korea, and therefore, many despaired and left for Japan for jobs and to escape the poverty at home.

Between 1939 and 1945, Japan forcibly brought many Koreans to the island to work under hard and inhumane conditions. For instance, they brought many young Korean women to Japan to serve as "comfort women," women who had to sexually satisfy the Japanese military forces. When the Allied forces defeated Japan in 1945, it was estimated that there were 2.3 million Koreans living in Japan. *(Lee 2008)*

However, many, especially the comfort women, lost their honor and had no option but to stay in Japan. Today, after fifty years of history, the Koreans, who comprise Japan's largest minority group, are not socially accepted. The Koreans in Japan occasionally are viewed as "problems" by Japan's sensationalistic mass media and have yet to be recognized as close neighbors who created and nurtured a unique ethnic culture. The Korean minority also suffers from discrimination in jobs, social welfare, housing, education, and social acceptance.

Koreans in Japan are not qualified for any benefits from the Japanese government, and women in particular suffer if there is no close family relative who can support them. Many of the elderly Koreans in Japan live alone, and an inability to access even basic welfare services have left many struggling to survive in their senior years. Interestingly, despite the discrimination, there are many Korean Christian churches in Japan who love to reach out to the Japanese people. There are many Korean pastors and missionaries serving in the Christian churches there that Japanese Christians visit. It is beautiful to see when the Korean and Japanese Christians worship the Lord together.

Only Christ can make two nations that were so hostile to each other sit at the table of brotherhood and love to forgive and be forgiven.

The Koreans in Japan again make a good example of how God anoints the colonized nation, in this case Korea, to reach the nation that colonized them with the gospel of Christ, just as the Hebrews did in the Roman Empire. Truly, they are blessed migrants.

Conclusion

You have read Blessed Migrants, including stories from those in the Bible and those who live today. However, there are many other migrants from different nations like India, Indonesia, or Central and South America that are as important as those migrants mentioned in this book. You have two possibilities: either you are a migrant or you are a host.

If you are a migrant, then I challenge you to build bridges and accept the nation in which you live. Learn the language and know the culture, but never bow to the worldly things that the hosting culture offers you. Live a life of dignity and integrity toward the native people. Never curse them with your negative words. Never speak evil of them. If you are a migrant who is going through tough times and/or heavy moments of adjustment, then remember what the Lord promised:

> Let no foreigner who has bound himself to the LORD say, "The LORD will surely exclude me from his people." . . . "And foreigners who bind themselves to the LORD to serve him, to love the name of the LORD, and to worship him, all who keep the Sabbath without desecrating it and who

hold fast to my covenant— these I will bring to my holy mountain and give them joy in my house of prayer. Their burnt offerings and sacrifices will be accepted on my altar; for my house will be calledthe house of prayer for all nations."
(Isa. 56:3-7)

God hears the cries of migrants. God accepts their prayers and answers their needs when they bind themselves to Jesus Christ, the Lord. Just like the Israelites in Egypt, they were a migrant people in a nation. The Egyptians enslaved and abused them, and God heard their cries and sent them Moses to free them. To today's migrants, the Lord has heard your cries and He sent someone greater than Moses for you—Jesus Christ. When you bind yourself to Him, He will set you free. He will bring you to the top and help you reach your dreams. I am a living witness and testimony of this fact.

As a migrant you have to understand that you have a double anointing; therefore, your prayers will be powerful and effective. Serve the Lord, and try to reach as many souls as you can. Preach to them not through words but through deeds and your life. You are not just a migrant. You are a God-sent ambassador to the nation in which you now live.

The hosting believers must realize that migrants are the doors to their nation's revival. Reach the migrants, and witness to them through your deeds. Help them if they need help; guide them if they need guidance. Do all you can to reach out to migrants and transform them from ordinary migrants into blessed migrants. Also, recognize and bless the existence of migrant churches and fellowships in your nation. When you do, then God will bless you and your nation.

By humbly uniting and working with them, God will bless your nation. He will break down the strongholds in your country and forgive the past sins of your nation. The Holy Spirit will visit your country. Remember that the blessed migrants are the children of Abraham, just as you are. Although they worship and pray differently, they all believe in the Lord Jesus Christ and the power of the Holy Spirit. Remember what God promised to Abraham, the Father of Nations and the great blessed migrant:

> I will make you a great nation and will bless you. I will make your name great, and you will be a blessing. I will bless those who bless you and curse those who curse you. Everyone will be blessed through you. *(Gen. 12:2-3)*

> Do not exclude them. Do not reject them. Remember Jesus said, "My house shall be the house of prayer forthe nations". *(Mark 11:17, NKJV)*

I want to close with this true story:

Every time I feel I am getting proud or I have to be humbled in my heart, I call upon a migrant. Most of the time, an African brother comes to the podium during the church service or a conference. Often, I choose the one who needs encouragement. Then, I take a bucket of warm water with a towel and wash the feet of this migrant. And as I wash his feet, I see tears falling down his face. Then, I dry his feet with the towel, and I tell him that God loves him and that he can make it, just as I made it. I tell him that I also have been where he is now.

I tell him that if I can do it, he also can do it because we both are the children of the Most High God through Christ and we both are the off-spring of Abraham. We are both blessed migrants.

Bibliography

Anderson, Allen. An Introduction to Pentecostalism. Cambridge, UK: Cambridge University Press, 2004.

Johnstone, Patrick and **Jason Mandrijk.** Operation World: 21st Century Ed. Carlisle, UK: Paternoster Lifestyle, 2001.

Lee, Samuel. Understanding Japan through the Eyes of Christian Faith. Second Ed. Lincoln: iUniverse, 2008.

Moll, Rob. "Missions Incredible." Christianity Today. March 2006. www.christianitytoday.com.

Overseas Filipino. Wikipedia. www.wikipedia.org. March 2008.

Pentecostal Power: a new poll sheds light on this fast-growing global religious movement.

Pew Research Center Publications. www.pewresearch.org October 2006

Yoido Full Gospel Church. www.fgtv.com. March 2008.

ti

www.ingramcontent.com/pod-product-compliance
Lightning Source LLC
LaVergne TN
LVHW020935090426
835512LV00020B/3370